Holy Places

The Golden Temple

and other Sikh Holy Places

Victoria Parker

www.heinemann.co.uk/library
Visit our website to find out more information about **Heinemann Library** books.

To order:
☎ Phone 44 (0) 1865 888066
🖹 Send a fax to 44 (0) 1865 314091
🖥 Visit the Heinemann Bookshop at www.heinemann.co.uk/library to browse our catalogue and order online.

First published in Great Britain by Heinemann Library, Halley Court, Jordan Hill, Oxford OX2 8EJ, a division of Reed Educational and Professional Publishing Ltd. Heinemann is a registered trademark of Reed Educational and Professional Publishing Ltd.

OXFORD MELBOURNE AUCKLAND JOHANNESBURG BLANTYRE
GABORONE IBADAN PORTSMOUTH NH (USA) CHICAGO

Designed by Joanna Sapwell and StoryBooks
Illustrations by Nick Hawken
Originated by Blenheim Colour
Printed by Wing King Tong, Hong Kong, China

ISBN 0 431 15512 7
06 05 04 03 02
10 9 8 7 6 5 4 3 2 1

British Library Cataloguing in Publication Data
Parker, Victoria
      The Golden Temple – (Holy places)
      1. Golden Temple (Amritsar, India) 2. Sikh shrines – Juvenile literature
      I.Title
      294.6'35'09545

Acknowledgements
The Publishers would like to thank the following for permission to reproduce photographs: Associated Press p. 10; Christine Osbourne Pictures p. 27; Circa Photo Library pp. 16, 17, 18, 26; Corbis p. 25; Dinodia Picture Agency pp. 9, 12; Gopinder Kaur p. 28; Harjinder Singh Sagoo p. 29; Trip/B Dhanjal pp. 20, 22; Trip/H Rogers pp. 5, 6, 7, 8, 11, 13, 14, 15, 19, 21, 23, 24.

Cover photograph reproduced with permission of Trip/H Rogers.

Our thanks to Rajinder Singh Panesar for his assistance in the preparation of this book.

Every effort has been made to contact copyright holders of any material reproduced in this book. Any omissions will be rectified in subsequent printings if notice is given to the Publisher.

Contents

Words printed in bold letters, **like this**, are explained in the Glossary on page 30.

What is the Golden Temple?

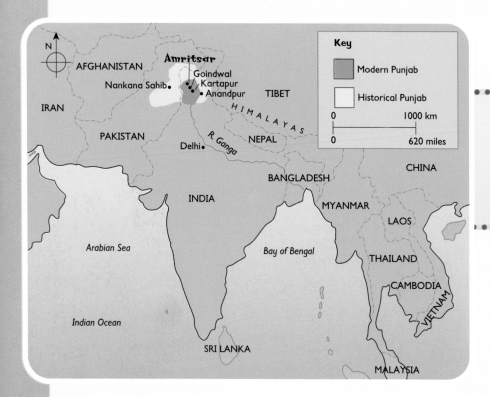

This map shows Amritsar in northern India

One of the world's most famous **temples** is in Amritsar, in the **Punjab**, north-west India. The temple's name is the 'Harmandir Sahib', which means God's temple. Most people just call it the Golden Temple.

The Golden Temple was built over 400 years ago in the middle of a **sacred** pool. People believed that the waters had powers to heal sick people. A splendid city sprang up around the Golden Temple, with houses, shops, schools and hospitals. This city is called Amritsar.

Other religions

Not all people in India are Sikhs. There are many **Hindus**, **Buddhists** and **Muslims** too. People become full members of the Sikh religion in a special ceremony. They share some food and a drink called **amrit**. This is to show that God thinks all people are important and that people of all religions should be friends.

Every year, thousands of people from different countries make long journeys to visit the Golden Temple. Some come just to look but many more people come to worship God there. They pray and do good deeds to help others. These men and women are called Sikhs, because they follow a religion called Sikhism. It was a Sikh leader, or **Guru**, who long ago gave instructions for the Golden Temple to be built.

The outside of the Golden Temple is covered with gold

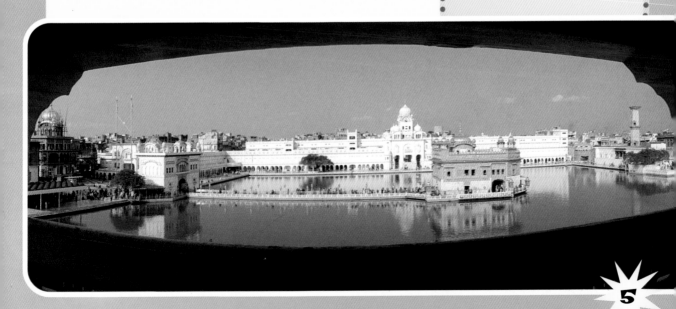

Who are the Sikhs?

Nanak thought that people of different religions should not fight but be friends

The word 'Sikh' means follower. Sikhs are followers of a **holy** man called Nanak. He lived over five 500 years ago. Nanak's family were **Hindus**, but he had a lot of **Muslim** friends. Stories say that when Nanak was about 30 years old, he walked into a river and disappeared. Amazingly, several days later Nanak walked out of the waters alive and well! Nanak said that he had been with God.

God had told Nanak that following a **religion** was not as important as living a good and truthful life helping others. From then on, Nanak was known as **Guru** Nanak.

Guru Nanak travelled around telling God's teachings as poems. One of his Muslim friends called Mardana wrote music for the poems so they could be sung as **hymns**.

Just before Guru Nanak died, he asked a man called Guru Angad to take over. Guru Angad wrote down Guru Nanak's hymns so no one would ever forget them. The next Guru, Amar Das, chose 22 women and men to travel as **missionaries**, spreading Guru Nanak's beliefs. The fourth Guru, Ram Das, decided that Sikhs should have their own city. So he built a town called Chak Ramdasspur. This was later renamed Amritsar by his son.

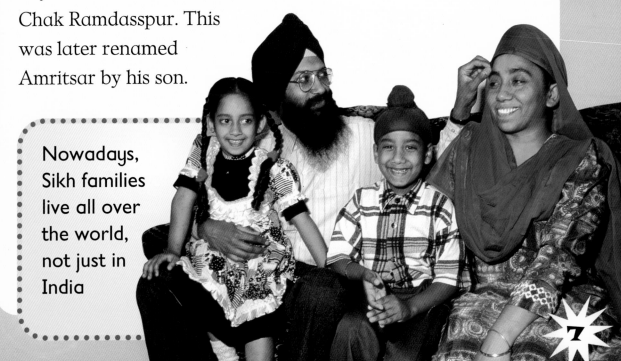

Nowadays, Sikh families live all over the world, not just in India

7

What is the sacred pool?

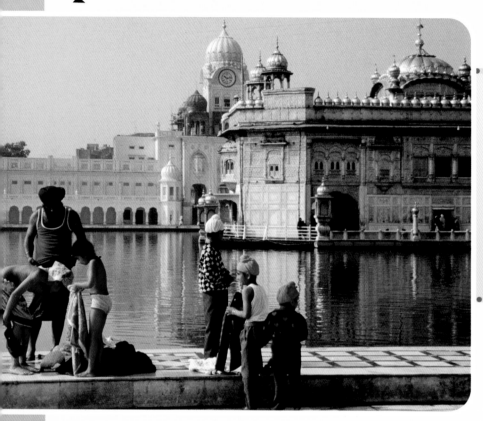

Visitors often bathe in the sacred pool before entering the temple to pray

People say that the land on which Amritsar was built was given to the Sikhs by a **Muslim** leader called **Emperor** Akbar. It is a special place for people of many different **faiths**, because of the **sacred** pool there. Sikhs believe that the second **Guru** had an illness that was healed with a **herb** that grew near the pool. **Hindu** stories tell how their god Ram was killed in a battle, but was brought back to life by drinking the water. **Buddhists** say that their leader, the Buddha, also once visited the pool.

DID YOU KNOW?

Sikhs speak a language called **Punjabi**. Amritsar is a Punjabi word that means 'pool of nectar'. (Nectar is a rare, sweet liquid.) The word that Sikhs use for temple is **gurdwara**. Gurdwara means 'at the door of the Guru'. Sikhs use different words for God. Waheguru is a name that means 'wonderful lord'. Satnam means 'eternal reality'.

The third Guru, Amar Das, thought the sacred pool should be made bigger. His followers dug it wider and deeper. Then under the fourth Guru, Ram Das, lots of Sikhs helped to build homes, lay roads, dig wells and open shops around it.

The fifth Guru, Arjan, made Amritsar look like it does today. The whole pool was lined with bricks and a mighty **temple** was built in the middle of it. This is the temple that today we call the Golden Temple.

This is how Amritsar looks today

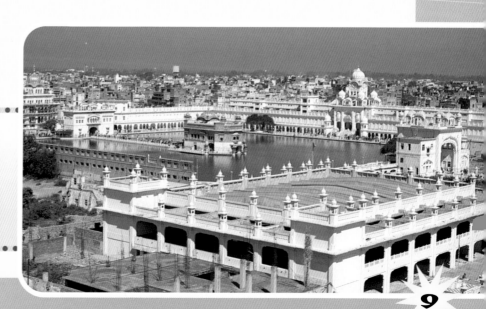

9

Amritsar after the Gurus

At the time of **Guru** Arjan, who lived between 1563 and 1606, the **Emperor** of India was a **Muslim**. He wanted the Sikhs of Amritsar to become Muslims. The next Guru, Har Gobind, moved away to try to stop the problems. But things grew worse. From then on the Gurus no longer lived at Amritsar. The tenth Guru, Gobind Singh, was the last. The trouble became so bad that he formed a Sikh army.

For the next 100 years, Sikhs were in a lot of danger. New rulers who wanted to kill the Sikhs took over India. At first, men and women fled from Amritsar. Later, they

This is one of the marble walkways overlooking the **sacred** pool returned and banded together in small fighting groups and built forts in the city to protect it. Many Sikh war-leaders built big headquarters called bungas. As the fighting stopped, the bungas became grander, like palaces. Important people such as scientists, artists and teachers came to stay at the bungas and study around the **temple** and the pool. The city began to grow and flourish once more.

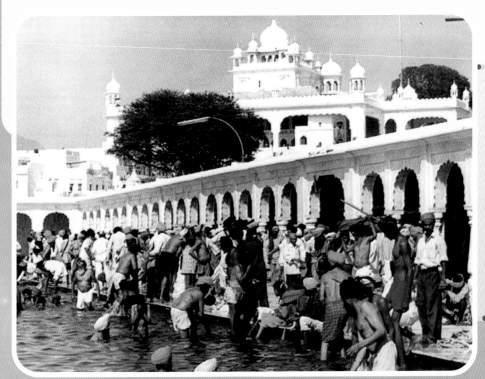

Visitors bathing in the sacred pool. You can see one of the bungas at the back.

What does the Golden Temple look like?

The Golden **Temple** is one of the most beautiful buildings in the world. The workers who built it were not just Sikhs, but also **Muslims** and **Hindus**. There are many carvings on the outside walls. A lot of the decorations have hidden meanings. Carvings of animals and birds remind Sikhs that life can be difficult at times. Flowers and fruit mean that life can be beautiful too.

The temple lies right at the centre of the **sacred** pool. There is a long, wide bridge that leads across the water. The temple has four doors, one on each side, to show that people from all parts of the world are welcome. Many Sikhs wash in the sacred pool before they enter the temple. They also take off their shoes and leave them at the entrance as a sign of respect.

Many precious and expensive materials were used to decorate the Golden Temple

Inside, the temple is decorated with more carvings, patterns in gold and silver, and beautiful wall paintings called frescoes. One room glitters and sparkles because it is covered in thousands of tiny pieces of coloured glass.

Every centimetre of the Temple is beautifully decorated

13

What is the Sikh holy book?

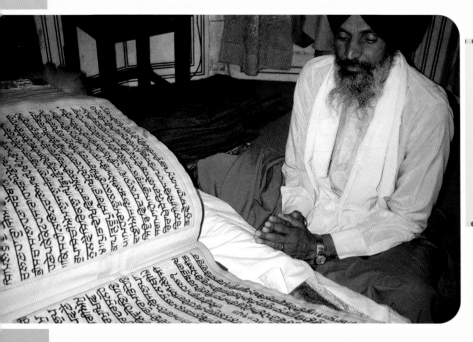

Sikhs show a lot of respect for their holy book, the Guru Granth Sahib

The **Guru Granth Sahib** is a collection of **hymns** written from the words of **Guru** Nanak by the other Gurus and **Hindu** and **Muslim holy** men.

When the tenth Guru, Gobind Singh, was dying, he announced that the next Guru would not be a man, but would be the holy book. It was given the title the Guru Granth Sahib. Sikhs believe it is the word of God.

Every **gurdwara** in the world has a Guru Granth Sahib. Each copy is exactly the same, with 1430 pages. When the Guru Granth Sahib is not being used, it is kept in a special room of its own and covered with a beautiful cloth called a **rumala**.

DID YOU KNOW?

This is the first verse of the Guru Granth Sahib, which was written by Guru Nanak. It shows that Sikhs see God as a spirit, who is not male or female:

There is only one God
Whose name is Truth
Who is the Creator
Who is without fear
Who is without hate
Who does not die
Who is not born
Who is the light
Who is known by the kindness of the Guru.

During a Sikh **service**, a man or woman called a **Granthi** reads from the Guru Granth Sahib. There are also talks to explain the readings. Sometimes the Granthi waves a fan called a chauri over the Guru Granth Sahib, to show respect. This sort of fan was used in the past in India to fan kings.

There is a special ceremony to carry the Guru Granth Sahib to and from the worship room

15

Eating together

At the Golden **Temple**, there is a big kitchen and a space for eating, called a **langar**. Every **gurdwara** in the world has a langar.

The langar has two uses. First, at the end of a Sikh **service**, everyone is offered a piece of **holy** food called **karah prasad**. This is a type of sweet pudding. It is made by cooks who say **hymns** from the **Guru Granth Sahib** while they are preparing it. Just before the karah prasad is taken to the worship room, the cooks **bless** it. Each Sikh cups their hands to receive a piece and they bow before they eat it.

Worshippers eating in the langar at the Golden Temple

Karah prasad

To make a pudding like karah prasad, ask a grown-up for help with these instructions. First, wash your hands. Then melt 200 grams of butter in a saucepan. Add 200 grams of semolina and stir the mixture for 5 minutes over a low heat. Mix in 200 grams of sugar and half a cup of water. Stir the mixture slowly until it thickens. Leave it to cool and set, then it is ready to share.

The langar is also used to prepare a meal that everybody shares after the service. This meal is also called langar. The meal is free and everyone is welcome, whether they are Sikh or not.

Guru Nanak thought that eating together was important because it showed that everyone was friends. Sikhs believe that in order to love God you must love all of God's people, no matter who they are.

These British Sikhs are sharing a meal at their own gurdwara

A day at the Golden Temple

Worshippers arrive at the Golden **Temple** at two or three o'clock in the morning. They sing **hymns** till four or five. Then the **Guru Granth Sahib** is brought from its resting place. Several Sikhs carry it in a golden box.

The Guru Granth Sahib is placed on the **takht**. A **Granthi**, or reader, lets the **holy** book fall open at any page and reads the first verse that appears. Sikhs believe that this is God's advice for the day. The worshippers say a special prayer called the Ardas, and **karah prasad** is given out to end the **service**.

Here, a Granthi is reading from the Guru Granth Sahib

Sikhs come to the Golden Temple all day. People read aloud from the Guru Granth Sahib. Worshippers sit and listen, then join others in the **langar** to eat.

Late in the evening, there is a final prayer ceremony. Then the Guru Granth Sahib is wrapped up. A Granthi carries it on his or her head to its resting place. The worshippers then clean and sweep the Temple.

Gurdwaras all over the world follow the same daily pattern.

The day's verse is written on a notice board so people can read it

What festivals do Sikhs celebrate?

Sikhs celebrate many festivals. Three important celebrations are held at the same time as **Hindu** festivals.

Baisakhi is held at Indian New Year on 13 or 14 April. Hindus thank God for the spring harvest. Sikhs celebrate how **Guru** Gobind Singh chose five men to form a special group called the **Khalsa**. These Sikhs promised to follow strict rules for the rest of their lives.

Holi is another ancient Hindu spring festival. Sikhs call it Hola Mohalla and celebrate it the day after Holi. Guru Gobind Singh decided that Sikh soldiers would celebrate it with competitions in

Many Sikhs choose to become a member of the Khalsa, like this man

Members of the Khalsa wear five things that begin with K. Kachera is underwear like shorts. A kara is a steel bracelet. The circle shape shows that God has no beginning and no end. A kirpan is a small sword. It reminds Sikhs to fight evil. Kesh means hair. Sikhs are not allowed to cut their hair. A kanga is a little comb that Sikhs wear to keep their long hair tidy.

horseriding, archery and wrestling. The competitions still take place today in a town called Anandpur.

Diwali is the Festival of Light. Hindus celebrate good winning against evil. Sikhs celebrate the bravery of the sixth Guru, Har Gobind. The Guru was once thrown into prison. When the **Emperor** finally released him the Guru said he would not go unless the other prisoners were let out too. The Guru cleverly saved 52 other people and returned to Amritsar in triumph.

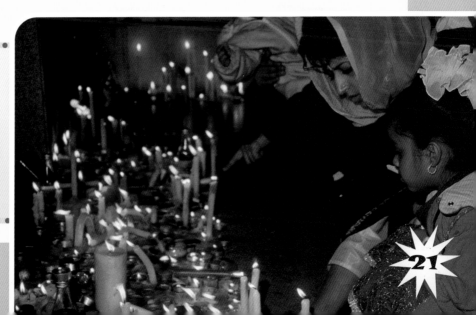

Sikhs and Hindus light hundreds of candles at the festival of Diwali

Sikh celebrations

Sikhs hold special celebrations to mark the birthdays and the deaths of the ten **Gurus.** These festivals are called gurpurbs. At **gurdwaras** around the world, people take it in turns to read the **Guru Granth Sahib** from start to finish. This takes two whole days and nights. The long reading is called an Akhand Path. Musicians play and worshippers join in with the **hymns**.

Hundreds of Sikhs get together to parade through the streets. Five people usually lead the way, to remind everyone of the first five members of the **Khalsa**. The Guru Granth Sahib is carried on its throne. It is decorated

These British Sikhs are celebrating a gurpurb

with flowers and banners and everyone sings hymns as it passes. The crowds are given gifts of sweets.

Special celebrations take place at Amritsar on the Gurus' birthdays and also on the day when the Guru Granth Sahib was first placed in the Golden **Temple**. The Golden Temple usually has silver gates, but for these festivals they are replaced by gold ones. The whole building is lit up outside. Inside, all the temple treasures are put on view for people to see. Thousands of Sikhs come to celebrate and huge feasts are prepared for them all.

Every gurdwara flies a flag like this one

23

What is the shrine of Baba Dip Singh?

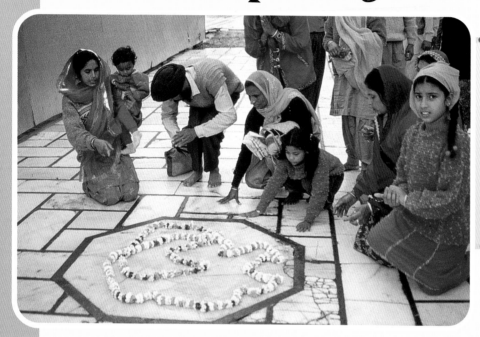

These Sikhs are showing respect for the hero Baba Dip Singh

The Golden **Temple** is not the only **holy** building for Sikhs in Amritsar. There are many other Sikh **shrines** in the city. An important one is the shrine of Baba Dip Singh.

Baba Dip Singh lived in Amritsar around 250 years ago. He worked writing out copies of the **Guru Granth Sahib**, which was a very skilful job. At this time the **Punjab** was ruled by the **Emperor** of India, Ahmad Shah. Ahmad Shah was a **Muslim** who did not like Sikhs. He did a terrible thing. He blew up the Golden Temple and filled the **sacred** pool with dead cows. Sikhs everywhere were horrified and angry.

DID YOU KNOW?

It is not only Sikhs who can worship in Amritsar. There are many temples for **Hindus**. Hindu temples are called mandirs. Muslims and **Christians** can worship in Amritsar too, as there are also **mosques** and **churches**.

Baba Dip Singh swore that he would fight Ahmad Shah's army and then rebuild the Golden Temple. Over 5000 Sikhs promised to help him.

Baba Dip Singh and his army fought their way to Amritsar to face Emperor Ahmad Shah. Most of the Sikhs were killed. Baba Dip Singh himself was badly injured. He managed to reach the sacred pool, but then he collapsed and died. Today, Sikhs place flowers on the spot where Baba Dip Singh lay. A shrine for him has been built nearby, and a light is kept burning there day and night.

A picture of the Hindu god Ganesh on a door on the Hindu Durgianna Temple

More holy places in Amritsar

Some of the Sikh **holy** places in Amritsar are not buildings. Many Sikhs go to a pool called Ramsar Pool. This is where **Guru** Arjan sat when he was putting together the **Guru Granth Sahib**.

Sikhs also visit a special tree at the Golden **Temple**. The tree is where Baba Buddha used to sit and give teachings. Baba Buddha was a man who knew Guru Nanak. He lived for such a long time that he was friends with the next four Gurus too. Baba Buddha was given the honour of being the very first **Granthi**.

The Dukhbhanjani Ber tree, near the Golden Temple

There is another tree in Amritsar that Sikhs believe is **sacred**. A story tells about a very poor girl named Rajni who came from a town called Patti. She lived before the Golden Temple was built. Rajni's husband was very ill so she took him to holy places all over India asking God to cure him.

Rajni arrived at the sacred pool of Amritsar, without knowing that people said it could heal the sick. She left her husband under a tree while she went to beg for food. While Rajni was gone, her husband bathed in the pool and was made well again! Sikhs call the tree where he lay Dukhbhanjani Ber, which means 'the tree that destroys sorrow'.

The Panja Sahib Temple where Guru Nanak taught

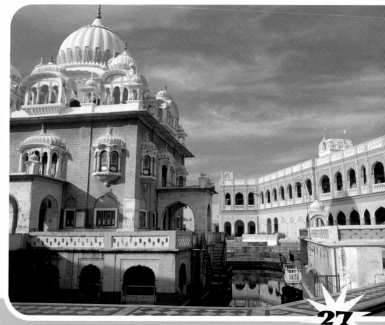

Everyday Sikh life

Today, there are Sikh communities in many different countries. Their **gurdwaras** do not always look the same. Some are specially built. Others are set up in old buildings like big houses. All gurdwaras have a worship hall, a room for the **Guru Granth Sahib** and a **langar**.

Sikhs all over the world worship in the same way. When they visit their gurdwara, they kneel before the Guru Granth Sahib to show respect. They sometimes take gifts of money or food. Men and women sit on the floor on different sides of the gurdwara, but they are on the same level and they have the same space. This is to show that all people are equally important. Children sit on either side.

This is the inside of a gurdwara in Britain

The gurdwara is the centre of Sikh life. Sikh families celebrate all their important events at the gurdwara. Weddings are held here. New babies are named in the gurdwara. The Guru Granth Sahib is opened at any page. The very first letter on that page is given as the first letter of the baby's name. A special event for boys also takes place here. Young boys keep their long hair tied in a topknot. When they are older, they go to the gurdwara for a special ceremony to tie their first **turban**.

This Sikh boy is taking part in his turban-tying ceremony

Glossary

amrit   special sugary liquid, which people drink in a ceremony when they become full members of the Sikh religion

bless   ask God to make somebody or something holy

Buddhist   person who follows the spiritual teaching of the Buddha

Christian   person who follows the teachings of Jesus Christ

church   building where Christians worship God

emperor   ruler of an empire, which is a large area made up of different countries and peoples

faiths   different religions, or beliefs about God

Granthi   man or woman who reads from the Sikh holy book and looks after it

gurdwara   Sikh name for a temple

Guru   Sikh teacher or holy person

Guru Granth Sahib   Sikh holy book, which is treated as a living person. It is also known as the Adi Granth (First Book).

gutka   shortened version of the Guru Granth Sahib containing the most important daily prayers and hymns, which Sikhs keep for personal use at home

herb   plant with a distinctive smell that is often used in cooking. Some are believed to have healing powers.

Hindu   person who follows the Hindu religion. Hindus worship many gods.

holy   to do with God

hymns songs sung to worship God

karah prasad sweet food that is blessed and given out to Sikhs at worship

Khalsa Sikhs who choose to follow the strict rules of the religion. These rules are also called Khalsa.

langar food that is free for all Sikhs who come to a gurdwara to worship. Langar is also the name given to the kitchen where this food is cooked.

missionaries people whose job is to travel and teach people about God

mosque building where Muslims go to worship God

Muslim person who follows a religion called Islam, based on the teachings of a prophet called Muhammad (pbuh)

Punjab place in India where the Sikh religion began

Punjabi language spoken by people in the Punjab

religion organized way of worshipping God

rumala special cloth in which the Guru Granth Sahib is wrapped when it is not being used

sacred something believed to be special to God

service organized gathering of worshippers

shrine place of worship that is special for a certain holy person or thing

takht throne where the Guru Granth Sahib is during worship

temple building where people worship God

turban length of cloth which Sikh men wear wrapped around their heads

Index

Titles in the *Holy Places* series:

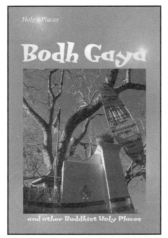

Hardback   0 431 15510 0

Hardback   0 431 15515 1

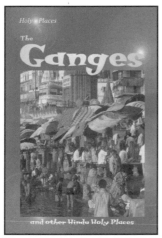

Hardback   0 431 15511 9

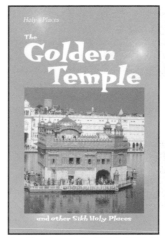

Hardback   0 431 15512 7

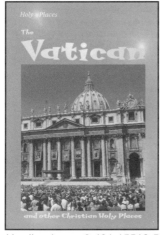

Hardback   0 431 15513 5

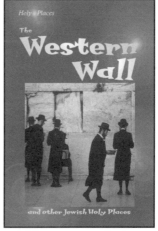

Hardback   0 431 15514 3

Find out about other Heinemann titles on our website www.heinemann.co.uk/library